Red Riding Hood's Sister

Red Riding Hood's Sister

Sarah Webb

Sarah Webb © 2018
ISBN: 978-0-9440-4880-1

Purple Flag Press, an imprint of vacpoetry.org
Design by Regina Schroeder

This book is dedicated to

the friends who took my hand:
Sheila and Mickey, Cliff, and Eddy

I: Red Riding Hood's Sister / 1
The Boy Who Came to Writing Club / 2
What She Saw / 3
Choose / 4
Because / 5
Leaving Home / 6
A Bride / 7
Good Times / 9

II: Dare Dance / 11
Self Portrait / 12
Advice to Young Poets / 13
The Man Whose Soul Rode Away on a Bicycle / 14
Open / 15
A Discussion of the Matter / 16
A Visit to the Old Town / 17
Ogre / 19
Dreams / 20
The Girl She Didn't Think She Was / 21
The Movie / 22
Airless / 23
Carny / 24
Morning Glories / 25
Making a Mistake / 26
She should tell him / 27
She ran / 28

III: She Fought with Bulls / 29
I See Her Now / 30
Caring What People Think / 32
White / 33
Clown / 34
At the Meeting / 35
If We Go Back / 36
What the Fox Said / 38
The Spartan / 39
He Explains / 40
Crying Wolf / 41
Taking in the Lightning / 42

In a Dark Time, Bodhisattva / 43
Keeping the Peace / 45
Driving Off / 46
Living Around It / 47
The Ones They Lost / 48
In Forest Dark / 49
Ceiling Fan / 50
Trap / 51
Russian Thistle / 52

IV: Out of chaos, the dancing star / 53
Monks: To a Younger Self / 54
Gently / 55
In the Body of the World / 56
Entering the Way / 57
Slow, Slow / 58
A Flower Folded / 59

V: Up / 60
Leaving / 61
A Beginning / 62
A Dream of Goblins / 63
Error Upon Error / 64
The Cuban / 65
From Ocean Deep / 66
Under Bear's House / 67
Lies / 68
Any Way Out / 69
Before Day / 70

VI: Swallowed Whole / 71
Wind Blows Through / 72
The Defender / 73
Changes / 75
The Day Her Daughter Was Born / 76
Turning to the Ordinary / 77
Leaving the City / 78

VII: Through Hills Dark With Trees / 79
A Basin of Water / 80
Lost / 81
And the Police Never Came / 82
The Island Where Monsters Live / 83
Left Behind / 84
Raising Her / 85
Gone / 86
How to Love / 87
911 / 88
That One / 89
The Voice of the Deep / 90
Hard Things / 91
On the Other Side of Cold / 92
Looking Back / 93

I

Red Riding Hood's Sister

This girl is going to be eaten by a wolf.
Her parents have warned her,
her friends have warned her,
that wolf has big teeth, he is up to no good.
But she said, *I must listen to my heart*—

which would have been all right
if she *had* listened—
but she didn't. She said to herself
I am in love, he is perfect for me.
Yes, he has been an evil
girl-eating wolf—but not any longer,
my pure love has saved him.
He will never eat a girl again.

She trembled, but she said to herself
it is because I want him so.

She shivered, but she said
it is because it is so cold in this forest.
Her feet started running, but she said
it is because I am so eager to see him,
and she turned back around.

When she saw him in the shadow of branches,
she felt a pain in her heart.
But, she said, *it is just the wild stories he has told me.*
When he took her in his arms and opened his mouth,
she said, *now he is going to kiss me.*

The Boy Who Came to Writing Club

When the girl opened the door that day
it was not the boy she saw standing there
(hint of Marlon Brando in the curve of the lip,
careless shirt over the worn jeans)
not the boy but her mother's warning:
Be nice to him—we're nice to everyone.
But he's not a boy to get close to.

Her mother had been his counselor at school.
What was the secret she wouldn't say?

His glance, the amusement in it,
the change in the air when he read his poem,
the girl supposed it started then—though when he called
to ask her out, she could have turned him down.
Her mother's lips thinned. *I will leave it to your good judgement.*
Oh, it's already set, the girl said. *We're going to the movies Friday.*

In the hall beside him at school, she caught whispers.
Communist, atheist, experienced with women.
He laughed when she told him.

Bear, she took to calling him,
and there was that about him, a glint of tooth
as he outraged teachers and his godly classmates.
He shambled through the day and clawed the walls.
Perhaps she wanted that, the walls shredded on her tidy life.

Still, she paused.
It was hard to push away the hands she wanted.

What She Saw

Perhaps she fell in love with him
because of how he saw. He had no camera yet
but the mind had already come
that one day caught the snow-whitened curve of hills,
the sister whirling in her winter coat on the track lanes
where they split, two futures diverging.

He showed her a poem—a young man walked through wind to a bomber.
She sat in the fragile light of the music that he played her.
How could it be, she wondered, this mind, this seeing?

In such a boy.
He played the beast, coarse and profane,
left a trail of shock and broken branches.

But when he fell silent...
there was something she sensed but could not say.

She watched him.
She saw where his eyes went—to the leaves pulled past,
to the rim of snow on the empty fountain,
to her face.

Choose

She fell
through black,
through light from windows in some small room.
She remembers it between the den and their parents' bedroom
—but wasn't the wall there blank?

She was happy when her mother called
said *fly home for break*
we'll celebrate your good start at the college.
She'd see them, see her dog and her brother,
see the boy after long weeks of letters.
Maybe her mother would make dumplings.

But it ended here in this little room
her mother saying *it wouldn't keep*
we had to talk to you
saying *your father and I, your brother*
saying *your brother tried to fight him*
for talking about you, dirtying your reputation
and that boy just laughed, lied
to get out of it, claimed your brother was drunk
that boy's a coward and a liar
your brother doesn't drink

and the girl ballooning
body bigger than the chair
could not think falling, only
but my brother *does* drink.
So you are going to have to choose
her mother saying saying
that boy or this family
not stopping demanding *which*
which do you choose
until the girl said *it will have to be the boy*

Because

She did it because he was as raw as flour
and she longed to cook.

The air vibrated with the drill of cicadas,
chipped dusty flecks onto the tennis court.
To the north the sky lightened and faded,
Prussian blue, no star.
A man drove past slowly.
He looked at them where they stood with their rackets lowered.

She did it because a lizard scuttered into the rock wall.
Promises hung in the air like the dark clouds—
I will love you forever.
It will be as if it never happened.

Would she do it again,
choose her mother's hysteria,
the questions she answered so carefully,
the clothes she packed and hid at a friend's house?

No, she wants to say, remembering all that followed
but she would, she would go on into the night, as she did,
taking the next step, and the steps later,
not knowing if any step would ever bring her freedom.

She did it because frogs form in spring pools.
She did it because the wind that night was from the north.

Leaving Home

She'd called ahead.
He'd said wait, but she couldn't wait.
She had to get out of that house or go as crazy as her mother.
Now with the fields going by—sorghum, cotton—
she couldn't believe she'd finally done it.
She had her best dress in the suitcase and her heels.
She guessed they'd get the license when she got there.
It got dark, but she sat up straight,
kept her hand on her purse with the money she'd saved,
and the guy beside her snored his beer breath into the night.
They stopped near midnight in Oklahoma.
At the counter, a guy with sweat in his mustache sat down close
but she ate her hamburger—she'd paid for it.
He kept looking at her, said something,
but she handled it. She'd have to handle a lot of things now.
At the stop the next morning she called her parents.
When she heard her dad's voice, it was hard.
At eight a girl from Iowa City got on.
They talked for two states about boyfriends,
the girl's volleyball team, working at summer camp.
She told the girl she was going north to see her grandmother.
She didn't say eloping, didn't say can't go back.

A Bride

She had just turned nineteen
when she ran off to the city and married him.
She carried a heavy bag for school from their apartment to the El,
rested it on her toes, cold in thin rubber boots,
and gave herself to the sway and clatter.

She walked to market with her aluminum shopper
like the kerchiefed wives with their blurred accents.
One time she slipped on the ice of the crosswalk—
oranges bounced over the slick gray.
A car turning the corner slid in a slow circle
but it missed her. She got to hands and knees,
one shin raw and the pant leg torn—money lost there to buy new.

She counted the dimes for bananas and round steak,
re-counted, nervous to stretch the money
from his job at the insurance company. What if he lost it?

Eventually he did, and there were scenes.
But this is before, when ladies in babushkas clucked satisfaction
as she scrubbed the windows of their garden apartment—
such a nice girl!

They had been married two months.
They saw a wall out the window, not a garden,
had ridden long streets on his sisters' bicycles to find rooms—
$75, money left over for hamburger.
The place needed painting, but it was big and warm.
They put a mattress in the bedroom and for their friends a sofa
and a long low table, plywood, painted Chinese red.

Sometimes she stood at the counter
in the steamy heat of the chop suey place
for clean white buckets of rice and vegetables,
sometimes she fried chicken (her mother had taught her that)
sometimes she opened cans. She was proud of it all—she was managing.

She was a bride, she felt that as she walked in the grocery store,
saw it in the smiles of the neighbors—*just married, eh,*
beamed the whiskered gentleman across the hallway.

People listened to what she had to say
and she could do so many things
now that she was a bride and had finally grown up.

Good Times

There were good times—the girl can't say there weren't.

There was going with Brian and Alice to the Rathskeller
and singing German oom pah pah with the families there,
the four of them eating sausages and waving beers

tiptoeing by Cezannes and Picassos at the Art Museum
and all the old pieces—Chinese horses, Assyrians carved with spears—
then sitting in the courtyard, cracking jokes in the spray of the fountain

riding the El in the slambang of the wheels,
her feet still cold from the snow but warming,
swaying with her hand on the pole, everyone city, everyone strangers

and after they'd left Chicago—burning their brakes out
on the logging cuts in the Oregon coast range, in a van
crammed with friends and cameras, chicken and wet flowers

falling asleep on the grass sloping west to the ocean,
with the sun on the girl's face and her friends around her on the blanket,
everyone quiet, the sound of the surf, a good day

at the base of a cliff, up from the stones and the waves, sifting
tiny tiny shells—spirals and wing shapes and delicate snails
so small she cupped them close to her eye to see them

drinking that night on the beach by a driftwood fire,
Walt blowing flame from the kerosene he lit in his mouth,
a great dragon tongue down the dark sand

walking the University campus in moonlight,
hearing an owl hoot as the boy took two-minute exposures,
the trees in the lamplight white as ghosts

synchronizing their watches to march en masse
to her cousin's house at the exact instant for supper, military time
(and hurting his feelings, which she hadn't thought was possible)

cats coming to nest at their heads when they slept,
tromping heavily over their stomachs the next morning to wake them,

and the way Prudence looked up at her, quizzical, from her yellow eyes

writing at her desk under the poster of dancing alligators,
with a teapot and a cat and stacks of paper
in a room full of windows, light from every direction

eating supper from a camp stove in the ice storm,
their coats on in the candlelight, his corduroy coat like an animal's pelt
soft and thick, half round her on the couch as they kissed.

There was so much.
The I Ching said it was not fate that turned it wrong
but the abuse of human freedom.

Yes, they abused it. And it ended badly.
But before that there was going down the river,
scraping over sandbars in the canoe the guys made from a kit

and there was snow, snow in the air, snow on the tongue
snow perfect and six-branched
all down the sleeve of his corduroy jacket.

II

Dare Dance

Chicken, they played, and Sling You Round Fast,
the break-bone blood-war don't-tell dances.
Those games flung him over the lip of the cliff
down shattering pine.

Head glued back, hand sewn on sideways,
still he kicked his way into their midst
into their wild, hard games
and did not think of injury.

The dance they danced—too far, too fast
the fire they leapt—too bright, too high
that dancing changed them all
but he alone fell burning.

He should not play, they said,
then, he should not have.
But their voices mattered little
to the wildest player of them all.

So on they danced
and as he danced, he fell.

Self Portrait

I.
He looks into the cold eye of the camera—
his own cold eye—

his shirt, starched flat, not yet
tucked into pants, no tie on the open collar

unready for the day
that demands so much of him.

Lines of lead, of green arsenic,
wind through his flesh,

cleave him with points of fracture.
He feels them scrape as he takes his pose.

His look says, I know what I am.
His look says, no one can save me.

II.
She had no self portrait.
He took the pictures—why should she?

In an early snapshot she stands slender,
laughing from the beams of a half-built house.

In another, skin coarse from scrubbing,
she has returned to wearing jeans.

She avoids the camera's eye, lifts a beer
in mocking tribute, sits uneasy in her heels.

Had she turned the camera to herself
would she have seen a maiden lost in forest?
Anything?

Advice to Young Poets

First point—everybody's got a story to tell.
It's just a matter of finding yours.
Of course, it may not have happened to you yet.
More likely, you just haven't noticed

like the girl didn't when she quit her first job
and the boy threw his bag in the car and went off.
Looking for work, they said. They didn't call it separation.

Each morning she'd write about dragons
and lament her lack of life experience.
At night she'd go to bed with a revolver under the pillow,
nervous that the cat would jump up and set it off.

Before he left they had a big fight.
He wanted her to call up the school district, beg to be rehired.
Teaching's just babysitting, he said, *but we need the money*.

He said, *I'm having to quit college because of you,*
said, *I can't trust you.*
He never could after that.

Which brings me to my second point—
no matter what happens, hey, you write about it.

The Man Whose Soul Rode Away on a Bicycle

His soul rode away on a bicycle
when he was twelve, he said.
Perhaps he believed that,
but he was no soulless man.
The murders he committed
were real murders. The lovers
he garlanded with necklaces, counted and caressed,
were real lovers.
He looked after that disappearing speck,
but I saw a bicycle in the weeds by our garden.

He mourned me, he said
because the girl he married was dead
and I the murderess.
I did murder her, that bright-eyed fool
who gave her heart for poetry and moonlight in a car
and only kept her soul because it was wadded in her pocket.
She deserved to be murdered. Such innocence is criminal
and if I had not done it, he would have.
That I could never have forgiven him.

Open

Take my wife shopping with you,
her husband pressed their guest. *Your clothes have such flare.*

The girl didn't need the lift in his voice to tell her.
The way he praised the roast she'd overcooked was enough,
the way he followed her into their bedroom and fingered her collar.
I know just the Riesling for the pie, he'd say
and leave with the woman to buy it at a special shop.
She didn't expect them back that evening.

Their story was that she didn't mind.
In the beginning she didn't.
How daring! the women cried in her consciousness group.
You're throwing off the chains of the past!

Her friend cocked her head at her. *I'm too bourgeois—*
I want my relationships closed tight. Are you sure?
The girl lifted her tea cup and smiled. *I'm sure.*

The glow of his attention lit the air.
The way he steadied, his joy—she could call it joy, couldn't she?
—that was enough. It's not like she wanted this for herself,
but to see that drawn face lighten…

A teenager afflicted with pimples and the awkwardness of high school
came to the door at the wrong hour for tutoring, stuttered.
A friend stopped calling, said, *I don't want to be in the house with him.*

At a party he sloshed his drink toward a woman on the sofa.
That one. Go over and make me a friend.
I won't do that, she said. *No.*

After they got home, after what they said,
she drove through neon from the shops.
Bars of red and blue hurt her eyes, but she could still see
the color, the rain on the pavement, could see
she wasn't—he wasn't—throwing off the chains of the past.

A Discussion of the Matter

*I may not be a one-woman man, he said
but you're always first in my heart.*

*It completes me, he said. Something
in me. Thank God for the sexual revolution.*

*It's different for you, he said. You don't
want it, you don't need it.*

*You don't, do you? he said. Is there
anyone you want? anyone you think of?*

*That's good, he said. I don't think
I could handle it. I love you too much.*

*It's different for women, he said. For you.
Women give their hearts. They can't let go.*

*I don't know what I would do, he said.
It could be very bad. I could hurt you.*

*I'm glad you don't want this, he said.
You don't, do you? You don't?*

A Visit to the Old Town

At a friend's suggestion
she went for lunch with Shay.
They made small talk,
how many years since she'd seen him.

He made a face at his coffee.
What is it? she asked him.
I'm angry, he said.
At Rachel? She'd heard they'd broken up.
No. You.

Me? She set down her fork.
Yeah, you. You know why.

She remembered her husband grabbing his gun, slamming to the car.
Some guy had come on to one of his women.
Friends at the party kept the two apart, talked them down.
It was Shay's house, and he got thrown into a door frame.
Did he think she should have warned him?
She hadn't, afraid the call would set her husband off.

She decided then about her husband—
he threatens but he would never actually do anything.

Shay's mouth twisted. *At Mt. Hood*
that weekend we all camped up there—
and when she still stared—*when I kissed you. You told him.*

How much later had that happened? a year maybe, or two?

The kiss had pleased her. Someone was interested in her,
like the women her husband saw. She thought then
it was something for both of them.
She still didn't want it but maybe someday, with someone.

Her husband had lain by her in the pulsing dark
and held her because the tent was whirling.
Had she told? even thought it a secret?
been that much of a fool?

What did he do? she asked.
Ask him. Shay scraped his chair back from her.

Ogre

I.
The ogre has put a lady in the cellar,
a lady who must drink her meal from a skull.
Her hair has matted and her eyes are filmed
and she has forgotten the day.

This lady, who used to love in the bright of the sun,
clings to the hands that thrust her down.
Give me a token, she whispers, *that you do love me.*
Sing me a song, even a song of teeth, of night.

Only the dank air answers.
Does no one love me? she sighs. *Do you?*
The eye of a rat gleams close
but she has left no crumb to give it.

When the ogre descends for wine,
her hands plead along his arm.
Do you love me?

II.
Other times she sulks.
I will not come out of this basement,
she announces, *until I am given my proper due.*

She was not kept there by an ogre,
though she believed so—nor punished for past sins—
though she thought so.

The door was always ajar.
She had only to open it and walk
into sunshine as blinding as dark.

Dreams

Each morning she looks at him sleeping,
watches his slow breath in and out,
as a mother might watch her child in his bed.
He has bad dreams
—or rather, he wakes into bad dreams
and he takes her with him
into nightmare landscape:
falling from heights, battling chitinous monsters.

With a word he can drag her
stone down into bluegrey depths,
a word like *slut*,
which he says calmly over breakfast,
his first word of the day,
and she knows what kind of dream
she will move in
this space of daylight.

She watches him at daybreak.
If he smiles at her,
if he talks over eggs and toast,
then she will live today in *her* dream,
the one that says
this is how it really is,
happy together.

The Girl She Didn't Think She Was

Was she angry?
Do not doubt it.
She stomped her dance,
a tall, proud girl,
spun round fast.

Dance close, she said
but not too close
or you'll get burned.

Was she on fire?
Oh yes, and all she touched
flamed black and bright.

Does she burn now?
Yes, endlessly
and lights the night
she sees around her.

And would I change her?
Not at all.
She is the light
that led me on.

The Movie

Jim and Julia came over, and the girl fed them spaghetti.
Afterwards they all went to a movie, something Japanese.
In the movie, a man—half mad—was living in a car in a dump
with his daughter, a child with luminous eyes.
He'd beg at the back of restaurants for rice for them.
One night someone gave him spoiled fish
and the child died.
Cans glittered away from them in the moonlight.
He looked down at the small body and howled.

After the movie ended, the girl's tears kept leaking out.
In the dark of the car, she wiped them with her hand.
Soon her face was wet again.
As she cleared the dishes from the table, tears
fell onto hardening tomato sauce.
After the boy went to bed, she stayed up,
drying the dishes, putting them away.
Tears dripped off her chin.

She sat on the sofa. The street quietened.
She saw the father's face with the moonlight on it,
the moonlight on the still child.
The salt in her shirt stung her breastbone.
Something hurt behind the wet cloth.
Her chest was breaking, rubble.

She took her purse, closed the front door, soft,
drove to their friends' house.
Their white faces came to the porch.
She lay in the bed they gave her,
tears seeping into the pillow.

She woke with her face dry.
When she went downstairs
he was sitting at their kitchen table.
What was that about? he asked.
She couldn't say.

She went home with him.

Airless

It is not the wolf
she burns to escape—
or not only the wolf—
but the heavy load of her heart.
Will there never be an end to its sighing?

Never an end to its clutching.

Unquiet, it stalks.
It will not sit, breaks any chair to sit.
It cannot breathe, its lungs are sodden dark.

She has filled with tears,
a bitter water moving.

The weight of it draws her down.
She sees the kitchen,
the table, her hand on the spoon,
through a wash of salt,
through eyes that have drowned.

Carny

Why these memories
of punk mermaids
at the all night carnival,
copper nipple rings
turning green from corrosive air?
The barker rasped the night with insults,
the Stones blared eight track
static fizzy on car
radio, shaggy heads
bounced to the music bingo
and she said *no* and *no* and *no*.
But she must have said *yes*
sometime, some spring
break, some wild
party night
yes to Jack Daniels and crawfish
red on carny sticks, *yes*
to lying down under bleachers
yes to her torn heart.

Morning Glories

When she laid plastic on the soil,
rain pooled in the dips, clear on the black.
Birds came to sip, did their fluttering dance.
She went along the rows with a kitchen knife,
slit the puddles to let water down.
She cut circles for peppers and rectangles for beans.

Morning glories sent long white snakes
seeking, seeking till they found an opening.
She stretched her arm in under clammy plastic
to grasp blind vines. Need sent them sideways,
deformed them, cave creatures sick for the light.

Driving down 20th Street each day
she passed a house she wouldn't look at.
She had to keep her herself from turning
toward that sun, toward any sun.

Making a Mistake

There can be no mistakes,
the man in the blue uniform told her.
You have used up your quota of mistakes.
There is no margin for error, he said,
tapping his pencil on the desk,
no time for erasure, no excuse for delay.
There is only one way to do it
and that is right now and without error
because we cannot go back for you
if you get off the train.

And when she finally did make a mistake,
a big one, there was another man
at a desk in the shout of steam,
and this one had a gun in a holster.
He looked at her cold and he said
If you hurry very fast and try very hard
you might be able to get on the next train.
You might be able to make up for that mistake
and then you will not have to die.

She should tell him

shouldn't she
how else could things ever be right

it had come again burning
a smiling face a lingering hand

furnace burning
hard in her chest breath rough
swelling in her finger tips

she scrubbed in the bath
red raw flesh

she used to have a wall to keep such things away
if she could step back
behind her wall she used to have a wall
he would hurt her if she told him
but there would be a wall

She ran

Fear had overtaken her,
moved her limbs for her,
heaved her breath.

She did not see or know.
Fear was as clear as moonlight.
Lightning stuttered.

A hand clutched her, a dark child
grinning, infected already
with the hate that seeks a victim.

I've got to go, she gasped.
My husband's going to kill him!

The boy crowed,
this fear wonderful to see,
the powerful brought low,
enemy half slain.

Her arm broke loose,
feet sharp on the pavement as shots.

III

She Fought With Bulls

She fought with bulls.
She fluttered the red cape like bravery
and leaped aside.
She fought with bulls.
They were laced with scars and vengeful,
they were massive as wrecking cranes,
they were ponderous, black and brutal,
and they sought her with mad animal eyes.
She did not know what she was doing
as bulls grazed by her.
She learned by stumble and mistake
and in the end she was gored.
And the crowd admired her and pitied her
because she fought with bulls.

I See Her Now

I see her now in a dark house,
dressing without the light so she won't disturb him
so she can feel her hands on the jeans
and the soft cotton of the tee shirt
as if she were blind.

I see her bathing in the tub
where she has painted a mermaid with flowing hair.
Her own hair floats around her in shampoo and froth
but she opens her eyes to the sting of soap
afraid he will enter and push her under.

She will not leave.
Every day she looks at the windows
if I had to I could leap through
I must remember to keep my arms over my face

The basement has no exit but the stairs.
He found her there as she loaded the washer.
He put hands to her throat his fingers were light.
There were no marks when he took them down

She wonders if it happened.

At night they press close. I see them lying at ease
breath as soft as dark through the summer window.
His hate stirs—she feels it flow toward her
green through the night air
She does not move. *Better that he not know I know*

She dreams she is dancing with a radioactive man
he is dying green shining
and because she holds him close
soft breathing to the music fallout
she too will die

and still she will not leave.

She sits on the side of the bed
her legs start running they chatter like teeth

He says to her in the emergency room
blood on her face and his face white
We cannot go on like this I will give you a divorce
He stands over her in suit and tie
only his cuff is bloody

Her head hurts when she moves it
No she says *no*

I see her in the garden gathering tomatoes
scarlet in the colander and beans green translucent at the edges.
She looks toward the house. She will have to go in soon.
Her mind is full of fog her thoughts dodge in the mist
He is waiting for his supper I will have to go in soon

Caring What People Think

A secretary at work cut her eyes
at the girl, whispered to her friend
that *she* would leave
right then at the first slap.
She would never take an apology,
she would never be weak.
What is it with women like that
she said, *where's their backbone?*

She didn't understand.
People are not going to understand
that love, or what you think is love,
can lead you slow into the tide.
A word, a sigh, a yes
draws you under.

In the grey dinge of the deep,
water is all you see,
every direction a dim distance,
sunlight a memory you doubt.
If someone had taken your arm, said *go*,
you'd wonder where.

Divers say there is a depth
below which you cannot rise.
Drift by slow drift you sink toward it,
the dark pulling down.

White

He advances
his face outside itself
a white coin like the moon
He laughs a witch's laugh
He swings the flashlight
arm raising slow, descending slow
bloody
In a cage of work dresses, sweatshirts
she looks out at him
He is lost into white, like static
like angels
She straightens, would come out, would face him
but his eyes, which have been white coral
suddenly see her
Don't, don't
a small boy cringing from her
don't leave

Clown

When the chiropractor turns her head,
she remembers a hand on her throat
and her breath catches.
So easy to give an extra twist.

Red slicked from her eye to the hard floor.
Her breath moved the dust beside his elbow,
his arm heavy on her.
Hands on her throat took her power.
Her husband paused a moment there,
pressing the windpipe.

Her palm squeaked across the wood,
to raise her, to let her
push and bite against that dark bag squeezing.
And as she twisted, she laughed—laughed?
and wheezed them both off guard.

She leapt, a clown with a red-dripped braid,
sideways stumbling, dancing.
Do you think I'm a grape
you just squeeze and eat?
No, I'm a cheese,
a cheese—and the cheese stands alone.
She spun, doorknob in hand,
his hand dark and surprised on her arm.

So drink a glass of milk,
she said to him, him
dark, looking out from the dark of the house
at her on the sidewalk in the sunshine.

The clown said nothing when she asked,
what now?

At the Meeting

Surely not.

The girl stared as the man who had been her lover
made his way through the people to her.
She turned from the hand he extended
but he leaned across a chair to her husband.

Can you come to the house? the man said.
We need to talk this thing through.

Talk! Her husband's face split.
A crack like a gunshot—the chair flew into the wall.
She stumbled back, let someone take her arm.

In the parking lot their car was gone.

The friend who drove her home turned the engine off.
Do you want me to come in with you?
Better not tonight, the girl said.

If We Go Back

If we go back from the night when he held a gun in his young wife's belly and she said, *Shoot*, we come to a day when they struggled on the floor and she was a monk who shouted *Free Tibet!* and he was facing a dog that had rushed him off his bicycle—

If we go back from the night that she was a witch, a bitch, how dare she! what did she think he was? we come to the day when once again his mother didn't cut his hair and it floated gold curls after him in the 50's backyard, his dog leaping and his airgun high as he ran—

If we go back from the nights when he cradled his Remington in his lap, click click squeezing off shots in the empty mechanism, we come to a night when she crept from the house, black-faced guerrilla to a low whistle and he spoke the words he'd learned from the drafts in a classroom on the wrong side of 15th and somebody said, *I shall have to call your mother*—

If we go back from the night when his finger tightened on the trigger and her face looked at him with eyes that didn't see him, we come to the eyes of the boys who ringed him on the playground and the jab of their elbows, and their hard arms hard knees pushing the breath out of him, and him biting, tearing—if he could just reach his knife—

If we go back from the night when he pushed the gun in her softness and she couldn't care any longer, we come to the night when he slipped through darkness into an attic where someone had stored things he hungered for and he prayed the strangers below would not wake as the gun exploded into view—

If we go back from the night when she looked at him and she was an owl, she was one bright eye, we come to the afternoon when he crouched in a tunnel and voices cried *weso! chinga tu madre!* and metal stung into his shoulders, bled down his cheek, they had his gun, oh God, they had his gun!

If we go back from the night when his eyes were darkness and her eyes were darkness, we come to the days when his mother didn't tell her secret but his father could count the months he had been in Europe. Go off to war and come back to somebody's bastard, shoes to buy for somebody else's brat—

If we go back from the night when she was a box closed tight against him and there was a secret, something she would never say, but she will! she will! we come to a night when he walked the street in a dirty tee shirt and a man looked up from the rim he was stealing and raised a tire iron and the boy fired—

If we go back from the night with his hand on the gun and her looking at him as if he were nothing, as if she could walk out the door and do anything and not care she was doing it to him, and he could stop it—stop it now!—with one squeeze of the trigger, then we come to the night...

What the Fox Said

A fox,
leggy with half growth.
Dark eyes glistened from the rust of fur.
Whiskers quivered at its nose.

It looked up at her
over the crimson of its entrails
where they had spilled onto the snow.

A tear in her heart
sharp as the tear in that belly
woke her to the dark bedroom,
the boy asleep beside her.

They had lain in the moon-shadowy room
and he had asked, *Are you going to leave?*
I don't know, she said,
though she thought she knew.

Waking, the moon gone
and those teeth white in her heart,
she couldn't say what she had thought to say.

How long? she asked the fox.
As long as it took to get here. The dark eyes closed.

The Spartan

When he stuck a gun in her belly
there was moonlight through the window
and she was not scared.
So pull the trigger, she said.
She was ready to die.

A teacher thought to save her suffering—
with grandmotherly kindness
he would chew the meat for her.
You, he said, *are the Spartan boy
who shoves his fox cub under the table
so his father will not find it.
He lets the fox gnaw into his stomach
and does not make a sound.
He will die.*

She did not cry out, though the teeth bit.
Home with your shield or on it—
she would not run,
she would turn it, turn it.

Do not hurt me, she whispers.

He Explains

I know I frightened you—the bloody paws,
the voice that turned to howl.
You fled from me,
never knowing if I'd come as man or beast.

Do I blame you?
Perhaps. I was a man still, despite the awful changes,
and you were sworn to me.

You could not understand how it rose up,
that urge to rend, to mate by force—
but I was ravenous and you were meat.

Luminous over the dark trees, a moon,
you called me out of cave and pelt
into the gleam of your round face.
But I could not take you down and gnaw you,
could not join you floating high.
I hated you for that, that shining,
and how you took yourself away—
left me dark in a cave in a dark forest,

me hungry for light, hungry for everything,
the man crying, *why doesn't she love me,
no one has ever loved me,* the beast growling,
come here so I can eat you.

Crying Wolf

He told such whopping lies—

that he would kill himself—
she would find him at the table
red seeping into the cloth
between the breakfast dishes—

that she would find her lover
slow revolving on a hook
in the basement behind the reloading bench

that he had spent one golden hunting afternoon
crouched upslope between ferns
scoping on the back of her neck.

No bullet took her
and the basement remained empty,
though her heart stopped
each time she descended the stairs

but that is why when she found him
with a girl in his mouth,
red seeping into the fur on his muzzle,
it was too late to call for help.

Taking in the Lightning

You can swallow lightning—
she knows. She has done it.
Some dark receiving ground inside the body
takes the blow
and meets it.

It is too strong to feel.
The world goes
and then returns.

Yes, you do die
but you re-form.
Now night is within you
and sky
and the wind that knocks down trees

all in uneasy balance.

Plants brown at your touch,
glass shatters to linoleum.
You shudder under blankets
when the branches shake.

Glare bright as sun
hides in your shadowing body,
coils inside and surges.
You must step carefully
or break apart.

In a Dark Time, Bodhisattva

He didn't hit her
It was coming.
Words like hammers.
Words.

She left by the front door,
said buy a paper.
Didn't cry.

Chamomile in the sidewalk crack.
Break in the sidewalk.
Break.
A car, that sound.
It didn't hit me.

Oak Street. Grand.

I could sit down on this wall.
I could.

Don't go by Ann's house. Danger.
Don't throw up.
Grass.
a little rock.
grass.
sign.

stand at the curb.
curb keeps you safe.
car car
light says green green safe light

newspaper. this is the newspaper thing.

There is a church
there is a man at the bus stop
and there is a car.
The faces laugh.
hungry eye.
The man in the car says

Car is gone. I have a dime.
I had a dime.
I have a dime and a nickel and
I need a nickel.
I need a nickel.
Kleenex fountain pen.
dime on the grass.

Car is back. Faces. Hard. Eyes.
The one at the window reaches his arm.
Says.
Arm doesn't reach. Quite.
I need a nickel, I say to him.

checkbook, fountain pen.
I have a dime.
I have a nickel.
I need a nickel.
Don't throw up.

Car is back.
Come here says the face.
We want to talk to you says a face.
Car door mouth

Car gone. Man from the bus stop.
Can I help you, miss?
A nickel for the paper. Can't find a nickel
I've read this one.
Paper folded neat.
Go home now, says the man.

Keeping the Peace

The girl stretched her limbs carefully.
No shouting last night,
all the last week—
the week before, too?

A survivor of the storm
crawling up the sand.
If she were careful...

They hiked on the mountain
with Jim and Julia,
good to let legs push, lungs breathe,
to be out among fir and larch.
They balanced over talus rocks,
thrust unbooted feet into
a rush of water melted from above.

She went to work, forgot
among telephones and chatter,
went to lunch with a friend—pastrami and rye.

If she were careful...
three weeks, four.

She made the bed carefully,
straightened the living room carefully.
She cooked, careful not to singe the edges of the bread.

When he came in the door, he pushed past her
and sat silent in the living room.
He didn't speak until morning.

Could she be careful enough?

Driving Off

She pulled in at a park,
a dark lot ringed with trees,
thick trees, a signpost by a narrow trail.
Not a safe place so late.
Someone could jump her here.

Oh, so was she going to be scared at that?
Her smile pulled to one side,
sour smile, stiff smile.

She slumped in the seat,
felt her breath slow.
A slap this time, that's all.
She hadn't needed to walk out like that.
They could get past this.

When she opened the front door
she saw relief on his face
before he looked down to his book.

Living Around It

The girl runs into a friend at the grocery.
They give my dad a week, her friend says,
but here they stand in the checkout line
to buy bananas and frozen pizza.
People have to eat.

Saturday the girl is pulling a string for her cat.
That morning she wrote on her book
(the boy showed up in it as an ice giant and a hero).
The boy walks through the room.

Sunday the girl cuts dahlias for the table
scarlet suns, heavy on their stems.
She sends him to the store for baking powder.
Their friends arrive, laughing, carrying baskets of hot bread.
In the tide of jokes, politics, tales of woe and triumph,
the boy and the girl tell an old story,
how they broke down in the desert and a trucker gave them a ride,
thirty miles to a store with a phone. They smile.
After the dishes are washed and their friends gone,
she makes a pot of tea.

The Ones They Lost

Isn't it that way for everyone, the friends gone?
Certainly it was for the girl and boy.
Sylvia to the Moonies, Al to stroke,
Susan to vodka on tranquilizer,
Ed to the drugs he thought would save them all.

Then Morrison to a night with a telephone book.
Drawing her finger down the names,
she whispered to the girl, *Can you find me?*

When Morrison's words broke, when she
wrenched the door and plunged between headlights,
her friends joined arms to hold her with them.
The boy manned a shift through the sightless hours
though Morrison hid from him and cursed him, only him,
cursed his cold hands, his cold, cold eyes,
called him Fuhrer, Goat King.
He never turned aside.

But now he is lost too, to deepening forest,
the fence posts down and night coming on.

In Forest Dark

Wolf, bear, giant,
there was something in him
out of an old tale
and in the girl too, the maiden.
Their track led through woods,
no crumb to show the way.
Wilderness lay close around
and in their hearts.

If he were bear, he loved honey—
she should not be surprised at that,
nor that he cared little for any law
that barred him from it.
She sought to restrain him,
got raked for her trouble,
lost that rope between the trees,
weak keeper to an uncaged bear.

She will not tell his secrets,
not the worst of them, not
where his cave lay with the bones about it.
When the firs closed their branches
and the moon darkened, she stood in dread,
fearing he might not return,
fearing what he might drag to her.

Ceiling Fan

I wouldn't give him air if he were in a jug!
her husband declares,
brooding over a business partner.
I hope he rots from the stomach out!

He sits in lotus to send harm to his enemies,
says, *shooting them would be quicker*
but they aren't worth the bullet!

He rages against a dog he claims has killed their cat,
returns one evening after an absence,
tells how each night for four nights
he stood in the shadows with a knife,
says, *one less trash dog!*

Therapy, she says to him,
abrupt over breakfast.
He looks at her. *Therapy!*
Any therapist that looked at me
would clap me in jail sooner than you could blink!
He grins. *And they'd be right.*

She lies in the dark, looking up at the ceiling fan.
It's up to her—who else can save him?

Vacuuming, she knocks against something
far back under the couch—the book he used for poetry,
filled now with notes in a cramped handwriting,
symptoms for poison, their recipes.

The blades of the fan chop the dark.

Trap

A friend warned her. *Your husband—*
you better watch out—he's walking into the dark.
I've seen him. Dark's all over him.

The girl said, *Oh no, you can't be right.*
He talks about dark, that's all.
She batted at the dark beside her napkin.

When she opened the front door, dark
flew at her. It slid down the sofa, inky.
She saw a line of it on his mouth.

Where did this dark come from? she asked.
He took her arm. Dark pressed from his fingers.
From you, he said. *Look how dark you are.*

He threw open her closet. *You can't hide it,*
he said. *Your shirts are full of dark.*
There is dark in your shoes.

You have to stop. You can't do this, she said.
Dark came and went through his eyes.
Dark grinned. *I will do what I want.*

His hand smeared dark down her face.
You make this dark, he said. *You.*
Try to tell, dark woman.

Russian Thistle

Globes of stickery arms,
tumbleweeds bounded across the highway
in the dust wind, wind from the north,
air dirty with sand, tumbleweeds
leaping and somersaulting in the cold.

In the lane ahead a tumbleweed crashed
into a car smaller than it was,
scored the paint, instant desert etching.

Dust filled their house, but the girl
didn't see the dark that had crouched there,
not any more than the usual dark
under the bed, in the back of the closet.
I went crazy for a while, the boy said.
It won't be coming back.
We'll be happy—you'll see.

She believed him about the dark.
But, happy.

A tumbleweed breaks at the root.
It waits then for wind.

IV

Out of chaos, the dancing star
    —Friedrich Nietzsche

At night in the ruined city
one building still stands.
Roofless, its walls tilt,
rough blocks
askew from its foundation.
Its pillars are thrown down.
Its shattered fountain
cups rainwater and rubble.
There you will find the star moving.

Monks: To a Younger Self

Once monks would flog themselves,
wear crowns of thorns, fast
and face the night alone.
Perhaps you are one of these, returned.
Not that you like pain—that old lie—
but that you will do anything
to join with your Beloved.

For Christ, they cut their arms,
let blood run,
and turned away from all that pleases.

And so have you.

Perhaps in the cold of Spanish churches
God came and filled their hearts with fire.
There they found all they sought
and were complete.

And you, can what you seek be found—
in a man, in a body of clay?
Or do you, like a wrongheaded old monk,
look outside for the light, blind to the flame within?

Enough. You will do as you do.
They lived too harshly, those old monks,
tried to force the door.
They lived long enough to find a different way
and so shall you.

Gently

gently
as one lifts a child,
she is held.

She feels the arms around her
in the early morning,
in the tired of afternoon.
Tender.

Why does it happen this way,
quicker than a breath,
stepping out of harsh words into quiet?

The angles of her body ease.
You, she thinks, *who are you?*

Tears come, sudden rain.

You I have called in the hour of my distress.

She walks in the evening.
The wind breathes the trees.

You, she thinks, *who are you?*

In the Body of the World

She is not sure what to call it.
Tasting? There is a taste to things:

the jar of the shovel into compacted compost

the softness of the rag on the jade plant
following the curve of each fat lobe,
spark of dust into air.

She remembers from her childhood
when she stood to feel the sunshine

the lift of grass in the wind.

She goes with a friend to a white-painted church,
sits at a wall in the plain room,
waver of wood grain under the white.

The hands, ready to fly up,
settle.

When she wakes, quiet in the morning,
an edge of dream:
a bird on a sill,
mountains, green waves of mountains.

Entering The Way

Light filled the room
her shirt, her hands cupping shadow.
She got up from her chair.
Yes, she thought. She meant she would follow.

But what to follow?
Not a church or a cause.
She felt a lift in her as she turned,
a current. It said *come this way*.

Later she wondered about the light.
How could such a thing be real?

But she remembered another time she'd met it.
Once when she was young and blind,
a light had filled the car. It asked *are you sure?*
as she pledged her life to the boy who drowsed beside her.
A dreadful mistake, that vow.

But this one? Ah, a long green road,
to walk the way, to keep on walking.

Slow, Slow

As a puddle fills with water
she changed by circumstance,
shining on a sunny day,
ruffled and dull in wind.

A girl who felt light moving—
aurora borealis—
in her and in the cracks of the street,
might scratch her face by nightfall,
yearning, despairing
at the life she'd built, the man
heavy and intractable.

Something in her may have changed,
turned on its path,
but the girl was prone to weeping,
hated herself for her nervous words,
the hands that startled to her face.

Slow, slow, she said as her heart raced.
Hold now, slow now.
Slow.

A Flower Folded

Petal by petal the flower of our heart
      —Amy Lowell

In the night room
at rest in her chair
she holds in, she sits bound

rosette
creased tight,
painful in its stricture.

Her breath swells
and subsides, swells
and in the darkness something loosens

a lace is untying, a bud is unfolding

petal by petal
unfolding.

The room reveals itself
bigger than expected.
What she sees in its shadow—

No. She cramps shut.

But again, again it is easing, again it is opening
look with the eyes of a mother
be kind.

Petals spread soft in the moonlight.
Around them, the air widens.

V

Up

Years passed, all water.
Drowned in spiraling current
she did not stir.

Her feet furrowed the sea grass.
Her fingers trailed anemone stalk,
barnacle filter, waving frond.
The quiver of water filled her,
the seashell roar of underwater falls.

Mermaids came in their quick fish flipping,
pulled and giggled bright around her.
Log-heavy, she could not dance.

What raised her?
One point of light, of air,
bubbled in her sunken body.
It moved her upward,
slow snail on a current of years,
past ledge and slope and coral,
out of the dark pull of the deep

to a dizzying rise and fall of chop,
bright slosh and the scream of birds.

Leaving

*For there is no one anyplace who isn't secretly departing,
even as he stays.*
      —Rainer Maria Rilke

She was leaving all those years,
rehearsing the smash
through the window with the chair,
the flight down the front steps.

Or, alternately, packing up one day
while he was at work,
taking the hidden cash,
the photocopy of her manuscript,
her movements increasingly frantic as
five o'clock neared.

But there was always some reason for delay,
one more frank conversation,
a plan to sell everything and move to Spain.
Stalemated, their talk
moved through the same sequences:
he says and then I say.
He hadn't hit her in three years,
that was progress, wasn't it?

One day he slapped her in the car.
Do that again, and I'll leave! she shouted.
He laughed.

A Beginning

Water rises.
It fills her throat.
Her hands scrape.

She sits in her chair,
sunshine on the table.
She does not stand.

Time to say
this is how it really is,
to lay down the mistaken banner,
to taste the truth
like ash in the back of the throat,
unwilling any longer to spit it out.

Black rises.
She lets its salt fill her mouth.
Yes, she says, *you are here.*

A Dream of Goblins

It wound beneath the sunlit landscape,
that dark way, and she did not know she walked it.

She filled her head with memory of sun and leaves
and wondered why she stumbled in an open field.
What could she do but amble on, puzzled
by shadows sliding past. Crows, she said, a cloud above.

And all the while goblins chattered their square teeth,
plucked at her dress with greedy fingers.
The one who led her spun her from their knobby arms,
lifted her, urged her up slopes of crumbling coal.
You cannot tarry—come.

Only when she slept did she see the rocky ledge beneath her
and hasten through the threatening darkness.
Only when she slept did she see the danger that she fled.

Error Upon Error

> *...she had lost herself long ago...*
> —George MacDonald, The Princess and the Goblin

Princesses fear goblins
and the dark insides of mountains
but something knew that the way led through them.
When it took her hand
it did not tell her of the road before her.
How could she have had the heart
to start on such a perilous journey?

But there was a road.
Mistakes and lapses nudged her toward it—
a mood, a whim
set one foot forward, then another.
She would not listen
to the dreams that came, the fears in the night,
and so she sickened—shook and fell,
cried out, wet with sudden sweat.
She said, *it is nothing.*
Nothing she would listen to.
Yet, step by step
she walked from that house.

Destined to be free.
Oh, it will happen, child,
though you grind your teeth
and pull back hard.

A girl can lose herself
and still be found,
lose herself and not be lost,
says the old story teller.

The Cuban

Because she was running herself
she understood the man's exile.
Soon she would have to leave
and there would be no returning.

When he spoke of his homeland,
how he watched it grow smaller
behind green sea waves,
she knew that sorrow.

He should not have looked back,
he told her. The revolution was lost.
He set down his pen.
My body remembers what they did to me.

You have a look I know, he said.
It is everywhere there.
His grave eyes watched her.
If you go, you can hold my hand.

From Ocean Deep

In secret seas
the scalloped mussels smack,
blue eyed and alive
in the salt green air.
Orange as their flesh
is your heart
with its own hidden tentacles,
hidden eyes.
It goes clacking through this kelpy street
through rain thick down as ocean
and its tears make it all salt.

Come alive, says the heart
though this salt ocean stings.
Come alive and I will show the way.

Hidden in the depths of secret ocean,
scallops drift and leap above grey sands,
blurred and distant as far ocean mountains,
a mile of twilight water round.

It is drowned dim here, it is watered pale.
But you? The tide creaks in your heart.
You can ascend to air—
bright orange of starfish,
the slap and splash of spray.

Jostled against barnacle, you may bleed red,
you may swim hard to make your way,
but you shall see the day.

Under Bear's House

Underneath Bear's house
there is a cavern like a root cellar,
cool for sleeping,
and steps lead down from that
to an underground stream.
It bounces over dark stones,
catches a glint from some opening ahead
where it will be freed from rock.

I could enter that water,
float along in its dark passage
unseen, an ape shine
pale as the crayfish with its trailing antennae
and as blind.
But at what cost?
What whirlpool, fall,
before that glimmer turns to freedom?

Or, I could climb the steps.
I could walk past the bear
and out the door,
claim that destiny.

Lies

Oatmeal is not oatmeal.
Toast is not toast.

Eggs are too tired,
poison you if you eat them every day.

She doesn't leave him because
she loves him.

And he would never really
harm her, would he?
He says not, says he
always loves her always hates her
thinks about killing her
would never hurt her

said he lied when he said he loved her
said he lied when he said he hated her.

After her lies, his lies
and all so turned against her,
she tells the truth now. Always.
Forces herself, like bitter medicine.

It's just that she is beginning to feel
things she can never tell him.
It's just that now she can't lie any more.

Any Way Out

It wasn't brave,
just the end of the road and every turn blocked.
It would have been good to have seen the light,
to be walking out the door because she believed in herself.

It wasn't like that. It was just one more mistake.
Still, the gate she blundered against clicked open.

It felt like rushing down rapids,
like a baby must feel when contractions start.
Leaving her husband for another man,
a married one at that. How embarrassing.

A friend told her it had taken three marriages to learn how
to leave with no one beckoning from the wings.
The girl had to do that later—think what was best
and choose, walk on alone.

But now it was scramble out anyway she could
when the one inside who called the shots
said, *enough now, it's time now.*

Before Day

the word binds
and she will not say it,
opening a window instead
to the dark woods

the birds have not yet begun to sing
the air is mild

she leans on the casement
as if she could hear
the leaves in their dark folding
the path that leads small
through crowding ferns

the bear rattles his throat
in a dream of fish

she must go now and light no candle
the house mute
no chair to plead, no coat to pluck

in darkness complete
she slips their hands

it is only a step to ground
from the dark hut
to the dark trees

she can go in this moment
before anything speaks
before bird call strikes

VI

Swallowed Whole

*Singing cockles and mussels
alive, alive-oh!*

When the girl stepped out of the wolf
she was as wrinkled and white
as Jonah.
Her eyes, milk clouded
couldn't take the sun
didn't recognize stores or cars or cash registers.

She thought the rumble of the freeway
was God growling.

But sight comes back,
eyelashes first and fingernails
then a down of brown
on an acid bald skull.

Alive, she said to herself
I thought I was eaten and gone
but I was alive.

Alive, alive oh, alive alive oh
She brushed her hair
and she sang, *alive
alive* in the belly of the wolf.

Wind Blows Through

The girl woke that first morning
to rain beaded on the windshield.
Cold crept in through her sleeping bag.

You can't live like that, said a friend.
We've got a spare bedroom.
So the girl followed her friend's Dodge
to an old two-story and settled into an attic room.
She slept and slept, went to work and slept again.

When she woke at last, even sunlight had changed.
Her skin felt scalded. Air dragged against it.
Clouds passed, branches lifted.

Too fast, too fast, the rasp of her sweater said,
the wet air as she walked at night, the words and
plans and coffee with her friend, with her cousin,
the shrill of the telephone and her friend's voice
calming the man on the line.

It sped and buzzed in her brain, all
this new life, new overwhelming the old.
Who knew where she would go, what she would do
and in the meantime there were traffic lights
forms to fill out, supper to help with.

A world that had slowed to standstill—
stuck beyond any shout or shove—
had begun to move.

The Defender

Coffee had never been her drink
but after weeks of it, the girl was getting used to the taste.
Her cousin brewed a pot the night she'd showed up at his door,
her hands cold though he was family and not afraid of much,
army man, Viet Nam.

I'm leaving, she had said. *It's going to be bad.*
Do you think you could...

Help you? he said. *I should think so!*
I've known you since you were two.
He put down his cup. *Hey, smile. It's a battle we can win.*
If we do this right, he won't set a finger on you.
Don't go back, he said.

She swallowed cooling coffee. *I haven't told him.*
I can't just disappear.
Her protector frowned. *You're not safe until you're gone.*

**

Her husband didn't raise his fist.
Nothing came but words—sweet words tumbling, troubling.
Don't you know I'd never hurt you?
Are you going to throw away all those years?
Come to therapy with me.
I was crazy the way I treated you,
but I'm not crazy now.

The boy crouched at the sofa.
Surely you couldn't mean to hurt me so!
His hands took her knees. His eyes went to the next room
where her cousin sat, alert.

**

Flowers and old photos, endearments on the answering machine,
friends who called to say, *he still loves you, he's heartbroken,*
still she kept her army of one.
Your German Shepherd, her husband snapped.
Don't you go anywhere without him?

One day she did.
Lulled by the long truce, she got into her husband's car.
He had a box of mementos to give her.
She had a letter saying goodbye.

He waved it away.
She set it on the seat between them and reached for the door.
Hear me out, he said. *Surely, it's not too late.*
She shook her head.
He grabbed her arms. *I'll make you listen!*

Then you'd better let go! Her knife-words loosed her.
She broke sideways out of the car.
She drove through side streets to her cousin's driveway
where she sat shaking.

The assault came then:
midnight phone calls, denunciations to parents
letters to bosses, cars that followed her.
She kept her door bolted.
They stayed up at night and tightened defenses.

Changes

She liked her new life,
so strangely different from her old.
She combed the paper for an apartment.
She and her friend—her best friend now—
painted its walls, put dishes in the cabinet.
They jump-started her car, peering at the diagram
and cheered when the engine caught.
They raked leaves on her friend's front lawn.

She went with her cousin for beer at a country-western bar
and rode their mechanical bull. A girl came on to her.
She spent an afternoon in her new place with her Cuban,
his touch so different from her husband's.
She found a bookstore and a bakery.

She called her mother and they talked and cried.

She felt dizzy from it all, so many changes.
The doctor sat at his desk,
dark against the light from windows.
He said, *No, it is not what you think.*
You're going to have a baby.

The Day Her Daughter Was Born

The day her daughter was born, it stormed.
The dark streets silvered.
The birth took a long time.
Her best friend held her hand
and the girl tried hard to breathe.
Her lover hurried in,
full of promises and instructions.

Hard work, bitter as cooking chocolate,
but the heart tore open and the child came,
a little Eskimo of a girl with her hair slicked straight
and her eyes dark as chocolate
looking at them, there.

Turning to the Ordinary

Eggs at breakfast, toast—
she must have eaten them but she hadn't noticed,
not any more than she'd felt the towels she folded.
It was the shouting that mattered,
the knock at the door at the wrong time of night.

After she left the dramatic—and the melodramatic—
behind with the record collection and her husband,
she fumbled for it awhile, remembering scenes
indulging in new ones, hitting the high notes.
But drama faded, and there was just 6 AM,
getting up to go to work, changing the baby.
Making supper—cheese sandwich and canned soup,
too tired to do more than that.

You can cultivate a taste for the boring—
what she would have called boring
but now was just life—reading the newspaper
pushing the baby in a stroller to the park

sitting on the sofa brushing her baby's hair,
soft brush in a soft stroke
sunlight on the cushions, apple juice in a cup.

Leaving the City

Her friend had driven the toddler to the park.
It was just the girl on the bed of the truck
and her cousin lifting boxes in the usual Portland drizzle.

When she'd run, she'd left behind the jade plant
and the rugs, her red shirt. Her books.
Some of it had made its way back to her
and there was new. She set a stroller
across a sack of baby blankets, soft baby towels.

Her cousin looked around the quiet street.
I don't see your ex anywhere, he said. *Do you?*
Unless you think he's going to jump out of the bushes.
She laughed. She *had* been eyeing the bushes.

The door snicked shut on the last carton.
A children's song jangled from her friend's sedan
as it pulled into the parking lot.

You won't have to worry so much about him,
her cousin said. *Not down there.*
She looked at the man who had kept her safe.
Thank you, she said.

Her cousin raised a coke in salute.
We may have lost Viet Nam, he said.
But we won this one.

VII

Through Hills Dark With Trees

Out of that hut one bright day
walked a girl
long held by curse in the dim interior.
Sooty and stained,
she stood at the gate.

She blinked at the rabbit
whose careless entry
had jostled a net of colored string
and broken the spell that confined her.

Where am I? she thought.

Then, *who am I?*
For she had come so long ago
one girl had entered and another left.

Miles around, the forest spread.
The giant's step had churned a track
but she could not choose that way.
She turned at random into shadow under limbs
lost and lost again.

A Basin of Water

The man she went to put hands to her throat too—
but with different intent.
Having known torture and the aftermath of torture,
he touched the back of his hand to her neck at her command,
removed it at her command.
He held a bowl between his knees
and dipped a cloth into the warmth of its water.
The cloth touched soft as he rinsed her,
soft over the place where she swallowed fear.
Wiping the memory away, he told her.
The memory will wipe away.

Lost

You cannot lose yourself
I answered.
*I—she—is in here somewhere.
She is watching you from across the sofa*
and still he said softly
You lost yourself
and I did not say yes or say no.

But now searching the house,
the medicine cabinet, the shed,
I cannot find her.
She is left behind on the road
and I reach for her, stricken.
She sits at some truck stop
with a sunburned guy, who, smiling too broadly,
puts his hand on her arm.
Or she is fumbling around the grass at the rest station
for something she thinks she has lost in the grass
and she won't look up when the attendant approaches.

She and a bony ribbed setter
someone dumped on the highway
are hungry and dull
but she doesn't expect to see me back.

How can I find her now?
She has taken to hiding when cars approach
and does not speak.

There are mountains between here
and the place I last saw her.
Still, I would go to her.
But I too have lost the way.

And the Police Never Came

I used to wait for the knock on the door
but no one came
to show warrant and badge
to say, *no more, you must stop
come along now*
so it happened again, again
and nobody went to jail

—not then.
They come now when I do not expect
with their *that's enough*
their *how could you have*
and their photos of victims.

I used to wait for the knock on the door
the dark figures on the porch
and the glint of a gun.
But they did not come,
not when red dripped the kitchen floor
not when I looked out the window at burning rain.

So I have made the city my jail
have walled off alleys where terror echoed
set grills to block slippery ways and steep.
Gates stretch now across many a flowered boulevard
with restaurants where ones I love
must wait for me and wonder.

The Island Where Monsters Live

Invisible, they coil among rocks
show transparent teeth.
They stalk the rock beach
devour sea worms, strain
the receding sea through baleen mouths.
They perch on the high rocks,
diaphanous, webbed.
Flies, salt mist, catch in the tents of their folds.

I have come to this island to find the truth.
It is an island of lies.
Lies open round me—holes in rocks
softness in sand.
I stand still, finding no place to set my foot.

The monsters shiver like sheets of cellophane.
They are dull, absent, but I will find them.
I shout, *I will throw you into the sea!*
I will trap you and kill you!

The monsters whimper, their claws scrabble.
I mutter, *No, I will not kill you.*

One beast, dark with age and scarred,
drags toward me, barnacles nest like lice
in the hollow of his coils.

His voice creaks seabird sour
he says, *Face me or you will never be free.*
Look about you. See,
the garden grows that you have planted.

And, truly, bees came to its flowers.
Its paths wound curving through the sun.

His eyes have wept red.
It might have been, he says.

Indeed, it is an island of lies.

Left Behind

> *that other one*
> *gone from me*
>   —Linda Hogan

I enter but she does not see me.
She is wearing a dress of wine-colored corduroy.

I am only beginning to understand.

Is the past a room we vacate
and all remains as it was?
furniture, evening lamp
girl frozen on the sofa,
chest hurting as she strokes a cat?

The mind catches her in flashbulb glare
eyes of a rabbit in the brights of a car.

Take my hand, I say
reaching down to one too deep to clasp it
one too deep in sorrow.

How can there be any saving her?

I say, *I am sorry for all I have thought of you.*
Will you forgive me?
She does not look up.

I sit beside her on the sofa.
Night is dark outside the window.
Wind rattles the pane.

I turn her hand, limp in mine.
Hear me, hear me, I whisper.
I am only beginning to understand.

Raising Her

I feel her hands on my forearms,
strong.
She wants to live,
she wants to live after all.
It is hard to raise her,
her dead weight of body,
but I hear her thrash and kick
against hidden water.
Come to me, darling, I whisper.
Again her hands tighten.

Gone

I miss him, my comrade.
He is lost in wilderness,
a dark labyrinth of trees.
Hate smoldered him like a fuse
and led him at length to that dark corridor.
Wolves live there, and heroes
and he is gone.

I miss him, shaggy bear, my comrade.
I reached into a pool bone cold and deep,
but I could not fish him free.
He cries in the night still,
stumbling between black branches,
and wonders where the light went.

I wonder too.
That gold that shone out from him,
how can such a thing burn out?

How to Love

I loved you.
People tell me, no,
it was only addiction,
only inertia,
but I see that picture Walt took of us
along a cold rush of water, mossy Oregon rocks.
You had your back to the camera
and you were fixing a button for me.
It felt tender.
It still looks tender.

You were wearing your corduroy coat.
Wonderful, that coat, bulky and soft.
I could hide halfway in it,
wear it with you.

I bought a corduroy coat this year.
I wanted brown because brown is my color
and black feels too harsh,
but I bought black anyway
because you had worn brown.

But there was a time when
brown corduroy meant soft things,
when your touch was gentle
and I did not shy away from it.
I don't know if I will ever understand
what I loved in you and what I feared.

So many women say they stay because
they love the man who hurts them.
Maybe we do.

A doctor told me one time
I don't know how to love.
But, you know, that isn't true.
I know how to love as well as anyone.
I just didn't know how to walk away.

911

A cry at the door—
Is anyone there?
the bell shrilling.
A woman pants,
white showing in her eyes
white falling from her bun.
A friend stands behind her in the yard.
Call 911!
we think he's going to kill her.
Her arm thrusts toward the library,
the figures locked there, man and woman.
The man's arm rises and falls.

Even in daylight the police car
stains the pavement *redblue redblue*.
Come now, I say to the woman.
I pull her to the curb beside me.
A line trails down her neck,
sweat and blood, pale red.
The man shouts guttural, strains
against the arms of the police, breaks free.
He stumbles to the corner of the building
before dark uniforms bear him down.
Under my arm the woman's shoulders lift, settle,
as the policemen push the man into their backseat.
It's going to be all right, I tell her. *It's going to be*
She says nothing.
I look down at the pavement with her.

Patent leather shoes. Gun in a holster,
smudge of mustache over unsmiling lips.
He holds his pad above us.
Name?
I feel the woman against me,
a stiffening bird.
The mouth grows harder.
We require your name, Ma'am.

That One

one...who will remain standing
      —Juan Ramón Jiménez

Lord of the house,
I've heard it called, and that one,
the one who is not lost
when everything has fallen

as things do fall,
our shacks of sticks and straw
cantilevered jackdaw over the cliff,
our oh so combustible A frames
in their brushy canyons.

You hope it will not come to you,
the fall, the fire,
but you are mistaken. It will.
I do not say this to wish you pain,
but when the fire comes,
all houses burn.

It is not the worst thing
to build from blackened stones,
from what is left to us

and if it has gone past
stone, past building,
then that one stands.

The Voice of the Deep

I have accused the girl:
she did not listen to her heart and so was eaten by a wolf,
she wasted the advice a dream fox gave her
and lingered within reach of danger,
she ignored the warning of her chattering teeth
and kept on walking, though the sea closed round her.

It is true she drifted down into an abyss almost past rising.
Eaten and gone, drowned and gone.

And yet.
It may be that she did listen
but the heart said something different
than you or I would say.
The road she walked took her under the water
but that is the road that brought her home.

Would we spare our children all difficulty?

Under the surface of every wave
there is a rising. We can say
the rock and mud beneath, we can say
the wind, the currents that circle,
the shifting deep, the moon

we can say, the traveler who stands calf deep
and lets the foam rise round her.

Yes, we hear a voice in the heart, and it can guide us:
Danger on this road—turn back!
But a wave may lift from a depth we cannot see.
In its surge we cry, passionate.
That deep too has a voice—a groan of gravel,
of water that carries our lives on its back,
a flotsam of sticks and weed.

When this voice spoke, what could the girl do
but listen?

Hard Things

Frozen ground.
The foot in a thin sock
hurrying across the yard.

Bone. Metal. The metal of a knife.
The way you looked at me.

Concrete and the dust on concrete.
Smell of places where people work but don't live.

The death of a dog.
Holding her when she couldn't stand.
Her fur under my fingers.

The mind muttering to vagueness.
Smell of shit in the nursing home.
Driving to see my mom, not wanting to go.
Going anyway.
Washing the dark from under her fingernails
into a bowl. The browning water.

Light on the lake, sound of my daughter's voice,
wondering if these things end.

Waiting in a truck in a cotton shirt
in the cramp of cold.

Holding against pain
it surges in, releases, surges.

Sometimes a baby, sometimes a death.
Sometimes coming into the house
and drinking hot tea.
I'm shaking but I'm warming.

Listening to the things you said.
Trying not to believe them.

Holding on until time to let go.
Letting go.

On the Other Side of Cold

Not just hard things
    —William Stafford

Sure, the breath tightens
when we wade into the cold river
and the child comes in a wild red surge.
Death—whatever it is—will find us.
But snow lazes on the wind in the milky light,
takes its time, falling up as much as down,
and I go out to meet it without my coat.

Looking Back

If we knew what would come,
would we dare?
to see the love turn sour,
the prices to be paid,
all to endure?

Is that why I slow,
venture less into the hills,
sit by the fire and do not
brave the dark?

And yet, though the way was stone
and my arms scarred,
much has come of all I lost
and what came at last was true

hard won and nameless
but my own heart's truth.

About the Author

Sarah Webb taught English at the University of Science and Arts of Oklahoma and for over a decade edited poetry for its journal, *Crosstimbers*. A Buddhist for many years, she presently co-leads a Zen writing group at the Austin Zen Center and helps edit *Just This*, a magazine of the Zen arts. Her poetry collection *Black* (Virtual Artists Collective, 2013) was named a finalist for the 2014 Oklahoma Book Award and for the 2014 Writers' League of Texas Book Award.

Teaching and publishing, raising a daughter, practicing Zen—this is a life the poet found her way to, but only after a hard start. The book in your hands tells the earlier story, when violence and mistake overwhelmed a young girl. Brought to a standstill, she turned at last to find a way out. This book is offered as a map to others lost in abusive marriage and to those walking away, making sense of what happened. May we heal.

Acknowledgments

Thank you to the editors and artists who initially published these or earlier versions of these poems:

Blue Rock Review "Under Bear's House"
Dragon Poet Review "The Man Whose Soul Rode Away on a Bicycle" and "Leaving"
Illya's Honey "The Ones They Lost"
Pilgrimage "A Basin of Water" and "Turning to the Ordinary"
Poets Bite the Bullet "If We Go Back"
Purse Ledger, Nita Pahdopony show at Leslie Powell Gallery "The Day My Daughter Was Born"
Rat's Ass Review "Carny"
Red River Review "Dreams"
Sugar Creek Review "Red Riding Hood's Sister"
Switchgrass Review "I See Her Now"
Waco Wordfest (earlier version of "The Boy Who Came to Writing Club")
Westview "Out of chaos, the dancing star"

CPSIA information can be obtained
at www.ICGtesting.com
Printed in the USA
FSHW02n0308250818
51509FS